# A Heavenly Place

Words of Inspiration to Bring
a Little Bit of Peace and
Paradise into Your Life

JACI VELASQUEZ
*with Thom Granger*

A FIRESIDE BOOK
Published by Simon & Schuster

FIRESIDE
Rockefeller Center
1230 Avenue of the Americas
New York, NY 10020

DESIGNED BY JILL WEBER

Manufactured in the United States of America
2   4   6   8   10   9   7   5   3   1
Library of Congress Cataloging-in-Publication Data
Velasquez, Jaci.
A heavenly place : words of inspiration to bring a little bit of peace and paradise
into your life / Jaci Velasquez with Thom Granger.
          p.      cm.
"A Fireside book."
1. Velasquez, Jaci.   2. Contemporary Christian musicians—United States—
Biography.   I. Granger, Thom.   II. Title.
          ML420.V326A3       1998
          277.3'0825'092—dc21       98-5431
          MN                        CIP

ISBN 0-684-84648-9 (alk. paper)
Permissions will appear on page 128.

# Acknowledgments

I'd like to thank the following people who made this book possible: my family, especially my dad, David Velasquez, my mom, Diana Velasquez, my brother, Dion, and my grandparents; Becky Cabaza and everyone at Simon & Schuster; Raul Mateu and the William Morris Agency; Thom Granger; and Mike Atkins, Pamela Muse, and Alleyene Sobel.

—Jaci

My thanks to Jaci for sharing so much of herself with me in our sessions together, that her fans and friends might gain insight and wisdom for their own journeys; to Mike Atkins for the opportunity; to Amy Dixon for transcribing the interviews; and to my family for doing so well without me while I worked on this project.

—TG

*Like everything in my life, I dedicate this to my Lord and Savior, Jesus Christ, and to all of you who are and who continue to be a part of me. You know who you are. This is for you.*

# Contents

# Introduction

*I think the hardest thing for me to deal with is my emotions and how I feel about things. It's not always easy for me to express all that I have bottled up inside me to others —or even to myself. That's why writing this book wasn't easy. I've been very honest about my life and why it's not necessarily a perfect one, though sometimes it may feel like a fairy tale or look like one from the outside.*

---

It seems like just yesterday I was a little kid, and the most important thing to me was who I got to play with and what games we got to play. There are so many truly important things in my life now, and as you get older, you'll begin to see what some of those things are for you. It's really kind of scary for me to share parts of my story with you, but I'm doing it for a reason: I'm still learning some important life lessons everyday, and I hope that some of the experiences I'm sharing here will help you understand your place in the world, and possibly help you and your parents understand each other a little better as well.

We all travel different paths as we journey here on earth, but our experiences as Christians facing challenges and celebrating life are quite similar. I hope as you read my story that you'll agree.

—Jaci

"I am not ashamed of the gospel, because it is the power of God for the salvation of everyone who believes: first for the Jew, then for the Gentile. For in the gospel a righteousness from God is revealed, a righteousness that is by faith from first to last, just as it is written: 'The righteous will live by faith.'"

—Romans 1:16–17

# CHAPTER ONE

# Taking Inventory

"I wanna be like no one's ever been before
And I wanna mean what no one's ever meant before
Get my hat on backwards-I'll be unique
I wanna be different-just like everybody else"

-From the song "I Wanna Be Different," by Bob Halligan, Jr.

*It's hard looking in the mirror sometimes, especially when you tell your-self, "Oh, my hips are too big," or, "Oh, my stomach's too fat." And you flip through magazines and you see these perfect, perfect creatures. You look at the cover of* Cosmopolitan *and you see Claudia Schiffer there with her perfectly thin body and beautiful hair and beautiful eyes and everything. Then you go home and you think, "Oh gosh, I look* terrible!"

I remember a time when I desperately wanted blue eyes instead of my brown ones. I have a friend who has big beautiful blue eyes. I'm never going to have those blue eyes. But you know what? You get over it. I like my eyes because they are unusually almond shaped. I think that it comes from my dad's side of the family. And I love my hair. I have great hair! But, there are still days when I would kill for big blue eyes. . . .

I started thinking critically about the way I look when I was probably eleven or twelve. Before that I could have cared less. But eleven or twelve was when it kicked in, and I started saying things like, "Oh my goodness, I can't wear this!" All of a sudden I didn't want to wear certain things because I thought they made me look fat. I became very concerned about my appearance and worried about whether I looked bad. Those kinds of thoughts can really get to you.

They sure get to me. But that can be a problem. If you're too hard on yourself, you can start to lose your self-esteem. You can lose sight of who you are and what you are. And it's all because you think you have to be something that you can't be—like me wanting to trade in two perfectly good brown eyes for blue ones. It's just not going to happen!

What's important is to realize and get to know who you are. I know that first I'm a child of God, second I'm a daughter to my parents and a sister to my brothers and sister, and third I'm a friend to others—and then comes everything else that makes me what I am.

One thing I've always known about myself is that I'm a very outgoing person. When I was little, I would just walk up to people and talk to them. My mother would always go looking for me because I'd just wander off and talk to strangers. "Hi, my name's Jaci. What's your name?" Here I am, three feet tall, and talking to everybody in the world.

Actually, I like being outgoing . . . mostly. I'm not self-conscious when it comes to meeting new people. I can walk up to just about anybody and say, "Hi, what time is it?" or, "I'm looking for this, can you help me?" But there is one drawback. I've always thought of shy, quiet people as being smart and serious. When I'm with someone like that, I wonder what they're thinking. With me, you always know what I'm thinking!

Years ago, when I was still attending public school—I'm home-schooled now—I would always try to act like I was shy on the first day of school. I didn't talk. It was *killing* me. I was dying inside! But I didn't talk because I wanted to look cool. I'd probably seen another kid acting that way, or I'd picked it up from a movie. Of course by the end of the day I was talking—I never could keep my mouth shut.

On the first day of seventh grade, a girl in my class was singing something, and she sounded good. So I guess I wanted to show her (and everyone else) that I could sing too. She was singing Whitney Houston's version of "I Will Always Love You," and I joined in. And she said, "Yeah, girl, you and me ought to get together." And I was like, "Oh, okay." So at the end of my day of being shy, I didn't just open my mouth to talk—I had to sing! I've always been a ham.

The flip side of my outgoing personality is that I actually steer away from deep conversations. I don't know why I do that. I guess I just assume that people expect me to be happy and fun all the time. Like when my friends ask me what's wrong, I will just say there's nothing wrong, just because I don't want to talk about it. I know that's something I need to work on.

Another thing I know about myself, that I know I also need to work on, is that I tell people what to do all the time. I'm so bossy. When I was little, I would make my friends in the neighborhood play with me, but I would be Cinderella, and they would be whatever. I would say, "You stand here. And you stand here. And these are your lines." I was the director and the star of everything! I always told people what to do.

I notice now that when I go out with my friends, I'm always the one who sets everything up. I make the plans. I make the calls. I'll find out which movie's playing. Everyone kind of looks to me and expects that from me. Lately I've been getting tired of it. And actually, I am dating someone who has that same tendency to be the leader. Sometimes we butt heads a little bit, but I'm starting to enjoy not feeling like everyone's looking to me for all the plans.

Everybody enjoys attention. I love it too, but lately, since I've been getting so *much* attention because of my music, I don't mind pulling away from the spotlight a little. When I go out with my friends, it doesn't matter to me as much anymore whether I'm the main attraction or not.

Still, it's hard when people don't like me. I went to a slumber party one time, and there were tons of girls there. For some reason I never knew, one girl, one of the "cooler" girls, didn't like me. And we got into this pillow fight. She had her fist behind the pillow, and she just hit me. I could not understand how this person, who didn't even know me, could not like me . . . and it hurt, in more ways than one.

When I was younger and did concerts with my parents, sometimes there would be girls in the back of the audience who would mock my hand motions (I use my hands a lot when I sing) or my dance steps. When they made fun of me, I would get so upset, thinking, "Why don't they like me? They don't know me and they're making fun of me?" Maybe it's that they were jealous or something, but it hurt me then, and things like that still hurt me now.

But I also know you can't live your life that way, always worrying about one person's opinion. Someone once said that in a crowd, 80 percent of the people are going to love you and 20 percent aren't going to like you. I get so worried about that 20 percent that I forget about the 80 percent! It's such a stressful thing, but you have to get over it or you'll drive yourself crazy.

I know I'm not a bad person, I just have things about me that I don't like. I guess every young person deals with that, but it's the *way* we deal with it that makes the difference. It's an easy trap to fall into, the trap of comparing yourself. Like, "Yeah, my hips look really fat, but that girl's hips are even bigger than mine." That's not fair—either to yourself or to the person you're comparing yourself to.

If I didn't like something about myself, my mother would say, "Remember you're made in God's image, so don't complain."

At first I took it literally and I thought, "Well, that's dumb. God's not even a girl!" But I guess I started to understand that God loves me and He doesn't look at the outside. He's not looking at whether my hips are too big or what color my eyes are.

Some people are going to look at you on the outside and be critical, but you don't really want those people in your life anyway. You want the people in your life who are going to care about who you are on the inside.

The people who are truly attractive are those who can admit, "There are still some things I don't like about myself," but yet they can catch somebody's eye with a look that says, "I'm confident about myself and I know who I am."

You have to know who you are—that's the secret. And you know what? Most people don't care if your eyes are blue or brown or green or purple. If you want others to like you, the first step is to like yourself.

*"For you created my inmost being; you knit me together in my mother's womb. I praise you because I am fearfully and wonderfully made; your works are wonderful, I know that full well. My frame was not hidden from you when I was made in the secret place. When I was woven together in the depths of the earth, your eyes saw my unformed body. All the days ordained for me were written in your book before one of them came to be."*

—Psalm 139:13–16

# CHAPTER TWO

# *Out of Control*

"How the mind can wander

How the heart can stray

Suddenly you're on the edge of darkness

How it makes me ponder

How I'm led away

Down a path that leaves me worn and tarnished"

-From "Shelter," by Mark Heimermann, Dann Huff, and Wayne Kirkpatrick

*Sometimes I feel like I'm on an emotional roller coaster. I'm a regular basket case. I switch from being happy and excited to just being depressed, for what seems to be no reason at all. I've always been emotional and dramatic. When I was younger, my brothers figured that out and would pick on me all the time, teasing me with things like "You were adopted!" And I would believe it and cry and cry and cry. I'm very passionate, and if there's something at stake that I believe in, I will just push and push and push until I get what I want. My parents might say, "No, no, no!" and I'll say, "You don't understand. I need this. I want this. And this is the way it should be."*

---

Anger is an emotion that can be downright scary. I remember when I was younger, my friends would come over to my house, mess up my room, and never help me clean it up. Drove me crazy. I hated that. And I hit my friend one time in a fit of anger—because she wouldn't help me clean my room! Sometimes I can't control my emotions, but there are right and wrong ways to deal with that. Hitting someone isn't the answer.

On the other hand, there are some emotions I may control too much. Like most people in my family, I never really cry in front of anybody. I get loud instead. Then again, sometimes I get quiet—too quiet—for all the wrong reasons. When my friends and I get into fights, if we don't talk it out right then, I give them the silent treatment. I am not going to bring it up again. The other person needs to bring it up. I'm bad about that.

Fact is, I don't even like to think about this stuff. I don't like to think about things I can't control. And I can't control my emotions.

I can't control the way I feel about things. Sometimes, out of the blue, I won't like somebody. I don't know why. They've never done anything wrong. I just don't like them, and I can't explain it.

The thing is, I *love* people. That's why I do what I do for a living. But sometimes the human stuff comes in and you go, "Ugh, what an annoying person. Go away," and those are the times you struggle with your feelings.

It's scary to talk about emotional things because when you trust someone with your private thoughts, you're sharing a special part of yourself. I know I trust my family, even though I really don't share everything I'm thinking with my parents. But there are not a lot of people I share with.

Part of that is probably just being a teenager. When you're a kid, everything you do revolves around your family. When you get a little bit older, you think, "I need my own space. I need my own place! I need my own telephone. I need my privacy."

But when people share with you, it makes you more willing to open yourself up to them. I have one friend who is so dramatic, it's just funny. She's more dramatic than I am! We're a lot alike. She and I, we just kind of blow up about everything, but we really click. It's great to be able to share your feelings with a trusted friend. And an honest conversation can be a good way to express your emotions.

Let's face it, everybody wants to be in control. I'm a control freak! But I'm learning that my emotions are a part of me that I can't always control. I think it's really interesting that the Bible lists self-control as one of the fruits of the spirit. We all want self-control, but it seems clear to me as I read the Scripture that without God's help, we're not going to be able to do it. Certain emotions can sweep over us without warning, pushing or pulling us in all kinds of directions. That's sort of scary, but I

36

think it's cool that God will work the quality of self-control into my life as I continue to learn more about Jesus. Now there's a guy who knew how to control his emotions and use them in the best way possible to help the people he loved.

*"But the fruit of the Spirit is love, joy, peace, patience, kindness, goodness, faithfulness, gentleness and self-control. Against such things there is no law."*

—Galatians 5:22–23

# CHAPTER THREE

# *Mi Familia*

"Jesus said, 'Go home to your family and tell them how much the Lord has done for you, and how he has had mercy on you.' "

-Mark 5:19

*My family has played the biggest role in shaping my life, guiding me and making me who I am. It's said that if you look at the people a person hangs around with, you can tell what that person is like. That's the way it is with me and my family. You can look at my family and know exactly what I'm going to be like, except for the fact that I'm a bit more high-strung. Okay . . . a lot more high-strung!*

It's probably because of the life I lead. And I'm so spoiled on top of that. I'm the baby . . . so everyone loves me. I get everything I want, and if I don't get it I get mad. But I'm aware of it, so, hopefully, that keeps it in check.

I have three brothers and one sister. My oldest brother's name is Mario. He is thirty now. My second brother, Julian, who is twenty-eight, just got married. And then there's my sister, Mindy, who is twenty-seven, and my brother Dion, who's twenty-six.

My oldest brother and my sister, Mario and Mindy, have a different mom. They're my dad's kids. Julian and Dion have a different dad, but they're my mom's kids. And then, when my parents got married, they had me, and now I've been blessed with a whole family.

I didn't grow up with Mario or Mindy, but Mario was around more than Mindy was. He was the short kid with red hair and freckles — an all-American-looking boy. But I didn't really get to know him very well as a little girl. He was around, but at the time we weren't really close. He was thirteen when I was born. It hasn't been until recently that he's become such a part of my life.

Mario's so easygoing—a lot like my dad—real quiet, really laid-back. You'd never know now that his life hasn't always been so easy. Out of nowhere, though I guess my parents knew, I found out he had problems with drugs. It was a tough time. But about a year ago he finally got delivered from drugs. He wasn't a Christian before, but now he is, and he's so on fire for the Lord, it's unbelievable. He's got his life together. I'm just so happy for him—and I'm closer to Mario because of the person he's become and the good qualities he always had.

My brother Julian is a tennis pro who has his own tennis club. We've always been close. I moved away from Houston when I was thirteen, but he lived with us up until then, going to college, doing all these things. But I always had a problem with his having girlfriends. Every time he'd bring a girl home I just couldn't take it. It drove me nuts because something was taking his attention away from me.

I understand now that when Julian is into something, he is completely into it. If he wants to help a person out with tennis, he will focus on that person like there's no one else in the world. So when he had a girl in his life, all he did was talk and think of and be with that girl. I hated that, because I wanted him to spend time with me, and I was just immature about it. I feel bad about it now—probably because I know what it's like to have someone special in my life! Now I see why you do that. You want to give all your attention to this person you care so much about. One of the reasons I love Julian so much is because he is able to give so much of himself. He's the kind of guy you'd like to marry.

It's hard for me to talk about my sister, Mindy, because I wasn't raised with her and I didn't know her well. I knew *of* her, but I never *knew* her. That was true of Mario, too, but I always had a special place in my heart for him. I guess I felt like Mindy never really gave me a chance.

She came to live with us when she was sixteen. But she never talked to me when I was little. I was just kind of . . . there. Back then I really thought it was cool that I had a sister, since I usually only had the boys around. But we never did the sister thing, though I would have so much loved for her to be closer to me.

Part of the problem has been that Mindy is never around. She's had her share of problems, even more in some ways than

Mario. But my dad sticks by her, through thick and thin. You can't blame him. She's his little girl. He loves her no matter what—like Jesus, really.

Now Dion's the biggest pain in the butt. But he's a good kind of pain in the butt. Dion has been the biggest rebel, but in the past two years he's grown up and has become such a man of God.

When he was a kid, Dion wouldn't do his chores. He wouldn't make his bed. He wouldn't do what my mom told him to do. So Julian, because he loved his brother so much, would go and make Dion's bed too. And then Mom would catch Julian fixing Dion's bed for him and both of them would get a spanking! I just love that story!

I've always looked up to Dion. I remember when he went off to college at Southern Methodist University in Dallas, we would go visit and I wanted so badly to be like him. In his sophomore year, he had his own apartment and a roommate. He was cool. He had great style in his clothing. He always had a cool house. One thing Dion didn't have, though, was a strong relationship with God.

Then Dion got married the day after he graduated from college. It didn't work out. He and his girlfriend lived together before they got married, and I think he lost sight of who he was. He seemed concerned only with making her happy. Dion has always appreciated the finer things in life, and he married a girl who wanted the same. She was a good person, but maybe she and Dion weren't ready for the serious commitment of marriage. Anyway, they ended up getting divorced, and Dion moved here to Nashville with me and my mom and dad. It was weird — Dion was the first to leave and suddenly, out of the blue, he's back home.

The day he moved here he found work. Today he's got a great job in the music business. He's set. And Dion's always loved the idea of being in the music business. He can't sing and he can't play an instrument, but he just loves music. And he loves God. And he considers me and my parents responsible for a lot of the positive changes in his life.

I've learned a lot from my older brothers and sister — from ways to live my life to things I should be careful of. I love them all so much, and I realize that being the youngest has its advantages when you have such good teachers.

My dad has been a Christian all his life. He comes from a great family, the fourth of ten kids. When he was a young man he started singing with a vocal group called The Latinos. He married Mario and Mindy's mother, but that didn't end up so well, and they got divorced. Then he met my mom. He was thirty-five and she was twenty-four when they got married. What a cradle robber! (Just kidding, Dad.)

One of my favorite things about my dad is that he loves Julian and Dion as if they were his own children. He never thought of them as anything else. They came to the house when they were just little boys, and my father immediately made himself their daddy. It's wonderful when someone can open his heart so easily. And the boys accepted him as their father in the same way he considered them his sons. I'm so proud to have such a good man for my father.

Dad was an evangelist up until I was two. He pastored for about four years, then got a job and did some normal stuff for a while. He hated it and went through a real depression when he stopped pastoring. Then God moved in his heart, and he decided to become an evangelist again and take my mom and me out on the road with him. I was nine when he decided to do that. He's still doing a little bit of that, but mostly he is being a dad right now, which I really appreciate. I can't depend on him to remember to pick up my dress from the cleaners—he's not a detail-oriented guy—but if he says he'll pray for you, he'll pray for you. You can always depend on my dad to be there for you when you really need him.

 $M$ y mom was raised in a Catholic home, the fourth of seven kids. She was a goody-goody growing up—and then she fell in love with a guy when she was fourteen, and got pregnant when she was sixteen—and married him. She had Julian when she was seventeen, and Dion came along two years later. She was divorced at twenty, and her first husband left her alone with two kids by herself in California, where there were no friends or family. She went home and lived with her mom for about a year and then got her own place in Albuquerque. She modeled for a long time. She also worked in a hospital. She did several things trying to support those kids.

Then, Mom met my dad when she was about twenty-four. This is the story of how my parents met:

My aunts Sandra and Theresa were going to this church, and they noticed that a group called The Amigos was coming to perform. They invited my mom to go to church with them (they'd been asking her to go for a long time). My mom said, "Okay, I'll go with you just to get you off my back." So she shows up at my aunts' church and sees these five guys on stage singing—The Amigos, the last of my dad's groups—and she thought it was the cheesiest thing in the world.

Meanwhile, my dad was up there singing his heart out, and the second he saw Mom he knew he had to marry her. She was gorgeous. Well, he went to meet her, and she did not like him.

But a week later, she found herself wanting to go back to that church—not because of my dad but because of the Lord. She eventually returned to the church about two months later and sat in the back pew. The next week she moved up to the second pew. Soon afterward, she gave her heart to the Lord.

The pastor of that church happened to be my dad's brother-in-law. Dad came back to the church to see if that beautiful girl was still there. He saw my mom again and asked her out. She said no. He asked her out again. She kept saying no. Fortunately, she finally said yes! They got married a year or so later. She didn't want any more kids. Dad wanted kids. They ended up having me. Surprise! They've been married for twenty-two years now.

My mom is the only person in the world who knows every single thing about me. (Well, except for a few things I'm just not sure I want anyone to know!) She's my best friend in the world, the one I can count on to keep my secrets.

Mom travels with me. We're together every day. Mom's the only person on the road who has nothing to do with work. I love her. She's a wonderful, giving woman of God. The difficulties she faced as a very young wife and mother made her strong and have made me respect her even more. Her experience has also strengthened my resolve about sexual abstinence.

So that's my family. I know that when a lot of people look at someone like me, they see the girl next door from the perfect family. But I don't exactly have a perfect family. The fact is, hardly anyone does. Everyone I know has got some sort of problems in their families. Or they aren't talking about it.

I think the quality that best defines my family would be our love for each other. Our strength, I think, is that we never give up on one another. We've had our share of ups and downs, but we don't look back. We forgive and move on. Every member of my family makes me love life for one reason or another. Having my mother along makes me love traveling, even when I don't feel like going on the road. My dad brought Mario and Mindy into my life, and he helps me see how loving them brings more love into my life. Dion makes me love myself when I don't feel like it, and Julian makes me love who I can be.

When I look at my family and feel the love my parents have for me, I see a glimpse of the way God loves me, the way he feels about every single one of His children. Like it hurts my mother so much if I tell her a lie—and I know it hurts God when I tell a lie. It hurts my dad so much when I say something unkind about someone—just as it hurts God.

But God can't come down and give me a hug. I need my family for that. Nobody loves me like they do. They love me for what I am and who I can be. They will always be there for me, and I will always be there for them.

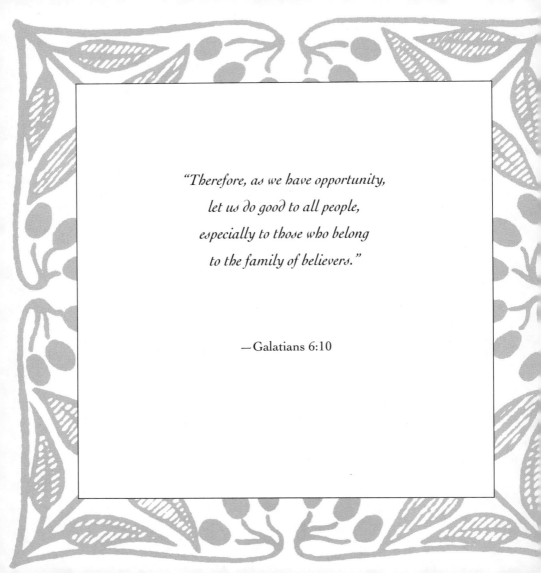

*"Therefore, as we have opportunity,
let us do good to all people,
especially to those who belong
to the family of believers."*

—Galatians 6:10

# CHAPTER FOUR

# Sharing Myself with Others

"Wounds from a friend can be trusted,

but an enemy multiplies kisses."

-Proverbs 27:6

*I've learned that you have to be very careful with good friends, because they are such precious gifts. Treat them well, because they can drift away and you'll never see them again. With family, it's different—you're in it for life, no matter what. But friends come and go.*

---

My first real experience with making—and losing—friends was with two girls from my old neighborhood in Houston. Our mothers had been pregnant on the block together, and we were all born around the same time. One of the girls was tall and blond, and the other was short with dark hair. But they were both very ornery!

Back then, my biggest concern was "Can I play today? I'm not grounded, am I?"—things like that. The three of us were constantly together, playing with Barbie dolls or having a picnic or whatever—and the next minute we were fighting. It was always them against me. And because I was never mad at just one friend or the other, I was always right in the middle of our fights. Major pain.

Then I moved to Dallas. I didn't really have a lot of friends there. When we moved back to Houston, I tried to hang out with my two old pals from the block, but we were all a little more grown-up at that point. We made our own friends and went in different directions. That's natural as you get older, I suppose.

When I moved to Nashville and started recording my first album, I really had a hard time. I didn't have any friends at all, and I was pretty depressed. But about the time we finished recording, I met a new girl, and she and I were like instant best friends.

We were inseparable. Either I was doing something to her hair or we were at the mall shopping. She spent nights over at my house, and I did makeovers on her. And then I met a guy on the 4Him tour, and his roommate, who plays for Michael W. Smith, and all of us became friends. All three of them are over twenty-one. I seldom have friends my age now. I think it has something to do with the fact that I have older brothers.

When all of us were together, it was a great time in my life. We were always doing stuff. Everyone would come over to my house, and we would rent movies, play games, just have a good time. I had never experienced such companionship before. I had never had so much fun. When people asked me, "How do you deal with giving up your teenage years?" I always said, "I haven't. Because I have amazing friends, and we always do things together when I'm home."

But relationships are fragile, and things change. My new friend and I were close for about a year, but then we kind of parted ways. And when she wasn't a part of my life anymore, neither were the guys. We had been a group. When we did something, it was all together—and it just wasn't working out that way anymore. The reason she and I drifted apart was because I had a new person in my life, a guy.

I guess I was hoping I could have a boyfriend and have my best friend too, but it wasn't happening. Because I was spending so much time with this guy, she wanted to be with us as well, and . . . that was weird. She'd ask, "What are you two doing?" and would get involved in our plans. I could understand that at first, but then I found out she was telling my boyfriend a lot of personal things I had told her. He asked why I wasn't telling him these things myself. She and I tried to keep it together, but it didn't work out.

It's a real hard thing to lose a friend and especially one you've entrusted so many thoughts to and shared so many good times with. We tried hanging out recently, and I invited her to a movie. But she's got new friends now, so we don't have the kind of things in common that we used to, and that's important. She's moved on, and I guess I have, too.

It's interesting how groups of friends sometimes make us who we are. When I was hanging around with her and the guys, I was talking like her and acting similarly to all of them in some ways. And I had never been one to go along with what other people are doing. Now I've felt the influence of having a boyfriend, but it's having a different effect than you might think.

I remember when he came over to my house in a big group of people. I had all my friends there—about twenty of us. He wasn't acting like the others. He was the leader of the group.

At first, it was strange for me — because I've always been the leader! He told jokes, he had the group's attention . . . he had the floor the whole time, and everybody loved it. I didn't have any other people in my life who did that, but with him I realized I didn't mind it. Maybe I've grown up a little in that way, or maybe it's something in him that helped me to let go of that need to be the center of attention.

I guess what I'm learning about friendships is how important it is to find people who you can really be yourself around and who are able to be the same with you. Besides my boyfriend, I do have two friends like that, and I'm very thankful for them.

I've known Kami since I was very little, and we've been friends forever. She has her set of friends, but we're still friends too. Kami is almost like a sister in my life, although more like a kid sister. She's the person I can talk to when I mess up, and I know that she's still going to love me anyway. She hasn't done everything in her life perfectly, so she realizes that everybody's going to make mistakes and is very forgiving.

I look at Christy as the responsible big sister. I respect her advice, and I look up to her in a lot of ways. She's a kind person, and she would be there for me if I needed her. Kami would be there, too. She'd be late . . . but she'd be there!

Kami is like family. She can drive me crazy at times, but I love her anyway. She likes to be in charge, and we usually do what she wants to when we're together. Kami's like me in that she likes to do things her way. And Christy's the other side of that. She'll generously do what I want to do and seems to know that there is more than one way to solve a problem. Different kinds of friends can bring out different sides of your personality. Kami and Christy have taught me a lot about myself.

I've learned that I'd rather have two really good friends in my life who love me as I am, instead of a bunch of acquaintances who don't really know me at all.

*"A man of many companions*

*may come to ruin,*

*but there is a friend who*

*sticks closer than a brother."*

—Proverbs 18:24

# CHAPTER FIVE

# The Dating Game

"The LORD God said, 'It is not good for the man to be alone.
I will make a helper suitable for him.'"

-Genesis 2:18

*Let me start at the very beginning of the whole boy thing. When I was eleven years old, I developed my first crush on a boy. He was four years older than I was. He was also my first heartbreak. When I turned thirteen, we started exchanging letters. By that time, he lived in California and I was living in New Mexico with my grandmother. We never even hung out. We were just pen pals, always writing each other. And suddenly . . . he didn't write back. It broke my heart. And I couldn't believe it. We'd been writing for so long. Everything was going so well. He wasn't my boyfriend, but he was working his way there. And he didn't write back. It was terrible.*

---

I saw him again. He likes me now, except I don't like him . . . like *that*. I guess it's always about a chase! It's always, "You like me? Well, I don't like you. Okay, I like you now.

You mean you don't like me back?" That's just the way it is, like some kind of game.

The next guy in my life lived near me. When we were eleven, he was in love with me, and I didn't like him. And then when I hit twelve, I started liking him, and he didn't like me anymore! I think it's just a natural thing in life.

I had my first kiss when I was fifteen years old. He was seventeen and a Calvin Klein model. He looked kinda like Antonio Banderas and had an accent like him too. He was gorgeous.

It happened in Costa Rica, the week of my birthday. I found out he had a girlfriend. In the course of a week, though, the girlfriend was out of the picture and he was flirting with me.

Isn't that weird? So here we are, I'm crazy about this guy, he's so good-looking, and he was *very* romantic.

He kind of tricked me into it. My friend told him that I had never been kissed before. So, being a guy, he had to conquer. One night we went up to the roof of the hotel. The view was amazing, the stars were shining, and I could hear the sound of the hotel's fountain down in the courtyard below. It was so romantic.

It was like a movie or something. He looked at me and said, "So you've never been kissed before."

And I said, "I don't want to talk about this! This is embarrassing." So we talked about other things — for a little while.

Then he asked, "Can I kiss you?"

And I said, "I don't know." I didn't know what else to say. I mean, I'd dreamed about this moment for years. Suddenly he just leaned down and he kissed me.

I wasn't kissed for two years after that. There were a couple of guys I liked during that time but no one I was really interested in.

Then someone special came into the picture. I met him after church one day, and we all went out to dinner afterward. We were talking (and I thought he was really cute), and I used this line to give him my number: I asked, "So you write some?" (We were talking about music.)

He said, "Yeah, I do."

I said, "Well, I'll give you my number. Why don't we write sometime?" To this day we've never written, but my plan worked!

Well, it worked eventually. He didn't call me for two months. Then I saw him again at church, and he said, "I lost your number. I put it on the back of a receipt and put it in my wallet. But I throw my receipts out every week, and your number was on the back of one."

So I said, "Okay, let me give it to you again. We'll get together and write." I thought he was just being polite. I didn't think he was going to call. But two days later he did. I picked up the phone, and I was so excited I started jumping on the bed. He came over to my house two days later. There was a big group of people over at my house, and that's the first time a guy I liked came over and was in the middle of everything.

I've always heard that a good way to get to know someone is with a big group around, because you never know, he might be a weirdo. At least in a group, you can get away from the person. So we hung out with this big group for about a month before we got together by ourselves. Fortunately, my new friend wasn't a weirdo!

I had never been on a date. I guess I had never really wanted to go on one. I had always thought that dating was such a pain. It just didn't make sense. I saw girls with boyfriends and that seemed nice, but I never wanted to date just for the fun of it. Maybe I was getting ahead of myself, but I guess that up until then, my attitude toward potential dates was "Would I marry this person?" not "Do I want to get to know this person better?" When I met this guy I thought, *I could spend time with him.*

Once I acknowledged that feeling, there were all these emotions rising up in me. I told a few of my friends about this new guy who was so kind, but I didn't tell them everything—I was trying to be cool about it. I did talk to God a lot about it, though. And He knew my heart. At first, I couldn't sleep at night. I'd never been that excited about anybody. So I decided to go out with this guy. Finally I could sleep!

I've been thinking about how this relationship, the closest one I've ever had with a guy, differs from that of a best friend. It's similar in the way that I feel like I can talk to him about everything. It's different because sometimes I don't *want* to tell him everything.

But it's a necessary thing to communicate when it comes to relationships. And I'm not very good at communicating like that. Suddenly I'm finding that I have to. You have to tell people what you're feeling, because if you don't, the relationship goes nowhere. It amounts to nothing.

My boyfriend is good about communicating. He's an open person. He'll get so mad at me sometimes and say, "Talk to me.

Don't talk around me. Talk *to* me." That's hard for me, but I believe God has sent me a friend who is teaching me to share my feelings, to not hold everything in. As I said earlier, I don't like to get into deep conversations, and with him I have to. I have to because we'll have no emotional foundation for a relationship if we don't.

It's important to me to have a real foundation for this relationship. Whether I marry this person or not, I have to look at him as someone I could end up marrying. If I can't do that, what's the point of dating? I know some people who go out with someone twice and they think, "Wow, I really like this person and I want to be with this person all the time." Then three weeks later they say, "Well, you know, I was just doing it to have fun. We weren't serious or anything." I don't want to do that. People are more important than that, and relationships are precious things.

" 'Cause I have seen the suffering

That loneliness can cause

When we choose to give our love away

Without a righteous cause"

—From "I Promise," by Jaci Velasquez and Johnny Ramirez

# The Fire Inside

"Flee from sexual immorality. All other sins a man commits are outside his body, but he who sins sexually sins against his own body. Do you not know that your body is a temple of the Holy Spirit, who is in you, whom you have received from God? You are not your own; you were bought at a price. Therefore honor God with your body."

-1 Corinthians 6:18-20

*If all human relationships are precious things, then there's certainly nothing more precious to me than the thought of a relationship that could involve my sexuality. To share myself sexually with someone is to share the most intimate part of myself—and to become what the Bible calls "one flesh" with him. Simply put, it is the act that consummates a marriage. And knowing that, I've made a promise to God—to stay a virgin until marriage. I intend to keep it.*

---

I made that promise when I was thirteen years old—to myself, to God, and to my parents. My parents had talked to me about sex, of course, and I knew their wish was for me to be strong in this area. But it was something I wanted to do too . . . for *me*.

I think too much of myself to give this most private part of me away to just anyone. I know if I save myself until I'm married, it's going to be especially meaningful. I want to have this first experience with the man I love and know that I'm going to spend the rest of my life with this person.

I don't want to give a part of myself to someone only to watch him drift out of my life. Every time you share yourself in such an intimate way, you're offering another person a part of your being, a part of your past, a part of your future.

Deciding to stay pure and keeping that promise are two different things. I made my promise when I was thirteen, before I'd ever been in a relationship. When you're in love with someone and feel the way I do about my boyfriend, there are times when keeping that promise is not easy. Sometimes we'll kiss, and it gets passionate. At that point, something goes off inside of me, and I stop. And I let him know, "Don't touch me in that way. I don't want to feel *that*. Because if I feel *that*, I'm going to want *more*. And I don't want things to get out of control."

It's never enough. When you kiss, you love that, and it's really good. Then you want something else. It's natural to want it, of course, but God has reserved that blessing for those who commit themselves to each other for life in marriage, which is a holy thing.

I know that it's easy to get yourself into situations that are very difficult to get out of. And I know that it's easy to blame guys for putting the pressure on to have sex. Let's face it, it would be great if a guy showed enough self-control to stop things before they began to get out of hand. Fact is, most times they don't, so the girl has to set the limits.

I know that for myself, and for most girls I know, the guy is going to do whatever the girl is going to do. She has to be the one to set the standards for herself and the relationship in this area.

What it really comes down to is being responsible for yourself—for your own body and your own choices. You can't blame anyone else for a sexual situation that goes out of control—unless you're talking about rape.

I think the best way to deal with sexuality in a relationship is to talk about it openly with each other before you ever get into the "heat of the moment." I did that with my boyfriend, over the telephone. We had a first kiss, and I noticed that I acted differently around him for a couple of days afterward. We were just very awkward with each other.

I thought about it and realized that we had crossed a small line—nothing that I really felt bad about, but one which made me realize that I was going to have to deal with this—and fast. So I told him, "Okay, here's the deal. You can't touch me here, or here, or kiss me like this, or be alone with me like this." Then the rules were on the table . . . and I wondered what he was going to say. The great thing was that he agreed totally, and we both felt better having gotten it out in the open.

But what if he hadn't liked what I said? This is the time when you have to remember the promise you made to yourself and God, and stick to your guns. It's not easy when someone makes fun of you for what you believe. But I don't want to get mixed up with somebody who doesn't share my convictions—and neither do you.

So what do you do if you find yourself in an awkward situation before you've been up-front about your intentions to stay pure? It's not easy, that's for sure. I know that I pray God will always keep me conscious of my actions. Conscious that when I'm doing something I might get caught up in, I can take a step back and look at myself and see what I'm doing. I've always prayed for that. I don't necessarily think about talking to God when I'm in those kinds of situations, but it sure helps.

The most important thing I can stress is to make sure the person you're having a relationship with wants the same thing you do. Because temptation will come, and if you've talked about it before, one of you will be able to stop things before they get out of control.

Now the really hard question, the one I get asked occasionally in letters—from Christian kids. What if you've already given yourself away and feel horrible about it. Will it ever be the same again?

The answer is yes . . . and no. One of my best friends has been a Christian all her life, but she's had some problems, and she's done a lot of things she shouldn't have. And I know that she asked God for forgiveness, and He has forgiven her. But we humans don't forget our past, and our sins and the sins of others will always be in our memories. That's why she has to forgive herself and make a promise to herself and to God that she'll keep herself pure until she gets married. She's done that, but is it the same as before she crossed that line?

I know I used to have romantic thoughts and dreams about my first kiss. But I wasn't consumed with lust over it—it wasn't real to me, just a distant dream. But that first kiss changed everything in my life, because once I experienced it, I wanted another kiss. And I would think it would be the same way with sex.

You can't be a virgin again. But you can be a virgin in your heart again. God can restore your innocence if you ask Him to, and the Holy Spirit will keep you in line if you ask God to help you keep your promise, as I have. I know God has someone set aside for each and every one of us, one special person who will bring us all the joy in the world. But we have to be willing to trust in Him to send us that person, and to wait.

*"So I promise to be true to you*

*To live my life in purity*

*As unto you*

*Waiting for the day*

*When I hear you say*

*Here is the one I created*

*Just for you"*

—From "I Promise," by Jaci Velasquez and Johnny Ramirez

# CHAPTER SEVEN

# Dreams Come True

"I will pour out my Spirit on all people.
Your sons and daughters will prophesy,
your old men will dream dreams,
your young men will see visions."

-Joel 2:28

*When I was a little girl, I had a dream of becoming a doctor. I guess everyone wants to be a doctor when they're little, or maybe an astronaut. There was a time when I wanted to be a lawyer, probably because my brother was in political science and he was studying to be a lawyer. I thought that would be really cool.*

---

I had other types of dreams—romantic dreams—where I wanted to be a princess and could only imagine what my knight in shining armor would be like. But I was sure he would take me to his castle, and we would live there happily ever after.

In some respects, I think my life has been quite a fairy tale. I started singing publicly when I was ten. When I was fifteen, I signed a contract with Myrrh Records and released my first album a year later. Every single from the album went to #1 on the charts. All these "dreams" really happened, and prayer has always played a role in helping me achieve my goals.

When I was seven or eight, I prayed God would send me a special dog. I looked in a dog encyclopedia and spotted the one I wanted, a Lhasa apso. A few months later, some people who had just gotten a Lhasa apso puppy were giving away their older one. They heard that I wanted a dog and gave it to me.

When I was twelve years old, I prayed that I would sing at the White House before I turned thirteen. And sure enough, on September 16, I sang at the White House, for the Congressional Hispanic Caucus. I sang "God Bless America" for the invocation, the prayer. A month later, I turned thirteen.

I know that some people would say that it's dangerous to believe that your dreams can come true. But the truth is, I don't think I've ever prayed for anything that hasn't happened in one form or another. I think that each and every time you pray, God looks into your heart and He knows whether those dreams are going to be good for you. And the things I prayed for—a childhood wish for a pet, a big dream of singing at the White House—were actually good for me. Seeing things like this come to pass has made God very real in my life.

When dreams become realities, it rarely turns out like you thought it would. Not bad, just different. Have you heard that saying, "Be careful what you wish for, you just might get it"? I think I understand what that means now.

The biggest dream in my life was to be able to sing for God, and it has turned into a reality . . . but not the way I dreamed and certainly not what I expected. I remember my family and I would sit and watch the Dove Awards telecast every year when I was little, and I just dreamed of being a part of that someday.

That dream came true. And along with it came the opportunity to meet so many people I've looked up to all my life—Amy Grant, Michael W. Smith—people who have been a part of my dream.

I did know what I was getting into as far as touring, though. I've done that for eight years full time with my dad. The problem now is that I have so much more at home than I used to that I don't like to be gone all the time. I have friends and family, and I have a real home to come home to! Sometimes I don't want to leave on the next tour, but I also know that, at least for now, I couldn't handle being home all the time, because I've been traveling all my life. I don't know anything different.

I never imagined how many people would be involved in making my dream happen. Where it used to be just me and my family, now there is a booking agency, management, a record company, so many people! They're wonderful and I couldn't do all these things without them — they're the team backing me up. But it's also a new challenge for me to be part of a large team like that. And it also has made me realize that sometimes you need a little help (and sometimes you need *a lot* of help) from the people around you to get what you want.

So my dream as a little girl, to be a singer just like my daddy, came true, just like a fairy tale — but it's not the way I thought it would be. Lots of little girls dream of being a fairy princess and living happily ever after, but the truth is they never live happily ever after. Just think about the fact that the princess wore a long gown all the time — sure, she looked great, but she never got to wear jeans and a T-shirt!

It's important for you to know that there's work involved in making your dreams come true, too. You can be all of the things that you want to be, with God's help, but He won't do it

105

all for you. Some people might think I came out of nowhere and started singing the day I recorded my album or something. But I worked very hard for six years with my family. We gave up our house when I was twelve and hit the road full time. We put our stuff in storage and got in our motor home and we were out—on faith. And sometimes that meant driving all day to go to churches where there were fifty people and walking out of the church with only $35.

So dream and wish and pray and plan . . . but be open to what God wants. It's not all going to work out the way you planned anyway. Lots of people who go to college and major in one thing end up doing something totally different from what they imagined in college. My brother, who majored in political science and English, now works in a music-publishing company. It never works out exactly the way you plan.

You can have your dreams, but be open to what God's dreaming for you. Because that's what's going to make you happiest.

*Could it be that He is only waiting there to see*

*If I will learn to love the dreams*

*that He has dreamed for me*

Can't imagine what the future holds

*But I've already made my choice*

*This is where I stand until He moves me on*

*And I will listen to His voice"*


—From "I Will Listen," by Twila Paris

# CHAPTER EIGHT

# Making Him My Own

> "The disciples came to Jesus and asked, 'Who is the greatest in the kingdom of heaven?' He called a little child and had him stand among them. And he said: 'I tell you the truth, unless you change and become like little children, you will never enter the kingdom of heaven. Therefore, whoever humbles himself like this child is the greatest in the kingdom of heaven.' "
>
> -Matthew 18:1-4

*I got saved when I was five. Some people would say, "How can you be saved at five years old? Saved from what?" I mean, it wasn't like I was a gross sinner or anything when I was five. But I think I did understand that it is important to go through that step and suddenly feel God's power and know that He's come into your life . . . and changed it.*

---

I was always in church. Growing up, we all had to go to church every Sunday. And because my dad used to pastor and my mom was a pastor's wife, nobody could stay home with me. So even when I was sick, I'd still have to go to church. That was just the way it was.

Church was like our home away from home, and sometimes that was hard. And as the children of the pastor, we were always scrutinized by some of the people in our church. They would look at us very critically, as if certain things were expected of us. My brothers were honestly the best-behaved teenagers in the church. But one of them was involved in drama and did a lot of plays at school. Some members of the church would ask my parents, "Why do you let your son do that?" Stuff like that used to drive me crazy.

In our family life we often spent our Saturdays going on church picnics. I hated church picnics. I always had to play with all the church kids, and there was this one little boy who would chase me around and try to kiss me. I just wanted to go spend time with my family on Saturdays, or go to the dollar movie theater. But we went to church picnics. I started to feel more involved when I got a little older and my dad encouraged me to start singing in church.

One of the first times I really remember thinking about God was when my church was giving communion. I remember wanting to be a part of it, but I couldn't take communion and I didn't know why. When I asked my mom, she said, "Well, you first have to understand that Jesus died for your sins and shed His blood and gave His body." Another time of communion went by, and I still didn't participate. This happened many times, and I thought very carefully about what my mother had told me and what I heard each Sunday in church. One day, I said to her, "You know, I do understand. I understand that Jesus is my one and only father and He is my God and He loves me. And I know He died for my sins." Finally, I was able to take part in this very special ceremony.

I've been a Christian nearly all my life, but it wasn't until about four years ago that God started becoming real to *me*.

When we're young people, it's easy to ride on our parents' relationship with God. But I decided I didn't want to do that anymore. I started realizing that my parents couldn't be accountable for what I was doing and for what I would do. I began to understand that I was accountable for my own actions.

I think this awareness had something to do with my involvement in Christian music. When the doors really started opening

for me, I knew right then and there that it was God's doing—
because music was always a dream of mine, and He knew.

Then things started changing, from singing in churches with
my family to going and doing my own concerts, then signing
my contract with the record company—and it hasn't stopped
yet! I started to feel that I didn't have enough to give people. I
started to feel that if I gave it all, I wouldn't have anything left
for myself—or for God.

I was constantly out on the road, doing so many concerts.
There I was, singing Christian songs, but somehow my relationship with God was suffering. Sometimes when you get
wrapped up in one part of your life, like I was, you forget how
simple it can be to stay close to Him.

I'd always read my Bible a lot. But what worked for me was that I started *talking* to God more, just talking to Him on a casual basis, not in a get-down-on-my-knees type of way.

I know now that my relationship with God is *my* thing. And I know that He's not just a being. I know that He's a friend, a friend who wants to talk. He doesn't just want to hear what we think He's supposed to hear. He wants to hear what we're really thinking, even though He knows. Being honest and open before God means that you have to search your soul. And talking to Him as a friend can be a good way to examine what's in your heart.

Most important, I've learned that He's *my* friend. Not my parents' friend whom I talk to because I'm supposed to. I'm learning that it's not what my parents expect from me or what the church expects from me that matters. It's what God expects from me that counts and what I can do for Him.

Some people think you're crazy if you say that God speaks to you. But I think God speaks to us all the time. I honestly believe that what the world calls a conscience is the still, small voice of the Lord speaking to your heart. I think He's giving answers we're not even aware of, unless we listen carefully. When I hear an inner voice saying, "I wouldn't do that," that's God speaking to me, and that's how I think He speaks to everyone.

Of course, I don't always *listen* to that voice. The closer I get to God, the more I realize how much trouble I could have avoided if I had listened more closely. I used to think, "I haven't really done anything bad. I mean, there was that time I spent the night at a friend's house and we snuck out. I felt really guilty about that." But I'm beginning to see that I've been a handful for God and my parents most of my life!

People have always looked at me as this sweet, innocent young girl who could never do any wrong. But I'm not perfect. I've done things I shouldn't have. I've lied to my parents—and that is so wrong. I know now that if I tell them the truth, no matter what I've done, they'll respect me more than if I lie. Our relationship will be stronger if I'm honest with them. And I know they will forgive me. And I think it's the same way in my relationship with God. The Bible says, "If you confess your sins, He is faithful and just to forgive your sins." But when we avoid talking to God about our sins, or try and hide from Him (as if you could), we separate ourselves from Him, and we're the ones who suffer. Every time.

Although it was hard for me to face up to the fact that I had a "dark side," it probably has helped me more than anything I can think of. It made me realize how weak I am without God and how strong I can be with Him.

On My Knees" has been my favorite song to sing every night. A lot of kids have come up to me, a lot of them PKs (preacher's kids), to say things like, "My dad's a pastor, and I've been raised in church, but when I heard 'On My Knees,' I just felt so blessed." It has that effect on me, too. Sometimes when the song is really moving in me, I feel a mix of sorrow and joy and I almost want to cry—because I think about my life.

Like the lyrics say, there are days when you feel like "letting go and soaring on the wind." But sometimes there are days in life when there's just so much junk going on, and you've done so much wrong, you've completely messed up. But know that you can still go before the Lord. He's right there, waiting. Know that you can still talk to Him. You haven't lost that capability. You haven't lost that privilege. You never will.

*"There are days when I feel the best of me is ready to begin*
*Then there're days when I feel I'm letting go*
*and soaring on the wind*
*'Cause I've learned in laughter or in pain how to survive*
*I get on my knees, I get on my knees*
*There I am before the love that changes me*
*See I don't know how but there's power when I'm on my knees"*

—From "On My Knees," by David Mullen, Nicole Mullen,
and Michael Ochs

# Epilogue

*Me, write a book? It still seems odd to me that I can write about my life and here it is for all the world to see and read in just a flash, but that it would take me a lifetime to know all of your stories. (Yeah, I mean* you, *the one reading this book!) What I've put down on paper is what is real and important in my life. Maybe I didn't write what you wanted to read, or what you may have been expecting. But you didn't just read about what my life* should *be — you read about what my life* is, *craziness, flaws, and all.*

Though I've shared some of my earliest memories with you and I've tried to bring you up to the present, this book has only captured a short period in my life. My life has changed a bunch since I finished *A Heavenly Place* and it seems to change almost every day. I know I'm different from most of you because of what I do for a living, but basically I'm a lot like you because I need and cherish my friends, family, coworkers, and most importantly my connection to the Lord. I find myself being pulled daily in one direction or another, but I know that if my world changed tomorrow, if the bottom fell out, I would just fall into that heart that has forgiven and loved me so many times.

Just the other day I had that amazing feeling you get when suddenly you feel so *alive*. It was a day where I experienced so many different emotions, so many ups and downs, and I felt as if I'd crossed a line and that my life would no longer be the same. As I braced myself for a particularly big challenge, part of me thought, "Oh no, not this!" But then I realized that I can't be afraid of what's in front of me anymore. None of us should be. Because that unknown place where we have to go sometimes is often where we find that special strength, that piece of heaven, right here on earth.

—Jaci

# Permissions